Lexicon

poems

Allison Joseph

Red Hen Press | *Pasadena, CA*

Book design by Collin Spinney

Library of Congress Cataloging-in-Publication Data

Names: Joseph, Allison, 1967– author.
Title: Lexicon / Allison Joseph.
Description: First edition. | Pasadena, CA: Red Hen Press, [2021]
Identifiers: LCCN 2020002086 (print) | LCCN 2020002087 (ebook) | ISBN
 9781597097178 (trade paperback) | ISBN 9781597098717 (ebook)
Subjects: LCGFT: Poetry.
Classification: LCC PS3560.O7723 L49 2021 (print) | LCC PS3560.O7723
 (ebook) | DDC 811/.54—dc23
LC record available at https://lccn.loc.gov/2020002086
LC ebook record available at https://lccn.loc.gov/2020002087

The National Endowment for the Arts, the Los Angeles County Arts Commission, the Ah-
manson Foundation, the Dwight Stuart Youth Fund, the Max Factor Family Foundation,
the Pasadena Tournament of Roses Foundation, the Pasadena Arts & Culture Commission
and the City of Pasadena Cultural Affairs Division, the City of Los Angeles Department of
Cultural Affairs, the Audrey & Sydney Irmas Charitable Foundation, the Kinder Morgan
Foundation, the Meta & George Rosenberg Foundation, the Albert and Elaine Borchard
Foundation, the Adams Family Foundation, the Riordan Foundation, Amazon Literary
Partnership, the Sam Francis Foundation, and the Mara W. Breech Foundation partially
support Red Hen Press.

First Edition
Published by Red Hen Press
www.redhen.org

Lexicon

ACKNOWLEDGMENTS

Poems from this collection were previously published in the following journals:

Atlanta Review; Kali Guide: A Directory of Resources for Women; GSU Review; Cream City Review; Eclipse: A Literary Journal; Alaska Quarterly Review; Southern Indiana Review; Tamaqua; Spoon River Poetry Review; and *Dogwood.*

CONTENTS

Lexicon

LEXICON

Let me taste the iambs on your tongue,
stroke you so your trochees tumble free.
Let me hear your anapestic pulse
stutter through the ribcage I embrace,
kissing every trimeter of skin.
Hear me whisper sapphics in your ear,
dangle dactyls from my curving lips.
You're no mere versifier but a bard,
making all my consonants come hard,
vowels so elongated in lust
my mouth's an instrument of luscious praise.
This poetry we make is evidence
that all we touch is figurative:
bodies pushing words beyond the real.

IF, WHEN, STILL

If no one hears you sob, would you still cry?
If no one hears your cries, would you still weep?
If no one hears you talk, do you still lie?

When everything goes gray, no lows or highs,
would you still walk upright, or would you creep?
If no one hears you sob, do you still cry?

When all your messages get no replies,
do you still write them down, or choke them deep?
If no one hears you talk, would you still lie?

If no one heard you laugh, or pray, or sigh,
would you still live your way, or would you sleep?
If no one hears you sob, would you still cry?

If no one answers you, will you still try
to write, content with what you reap?
If no one hears you talk, do you still lie?

When no one's close to hear your alibis,
would you still make them up, however cheap?
If no one hears you sob, would you still cry?
If no one hears you talk, do you still lie?

DREAMING THE SPECTRUM

My bones are hard ivory,
eyes blacker than ebony wood.
Luscious russet grapes consume me,
and I them; I eat olives, avoid cactus.
Gold coins entice, but bananas do too,
and mangoes that blush ripe as if lipstick-painted.
I dance the little flames of popsicles
into my mouth, scarf down magenta cherries.
My skin, more caramel than leather,
feels the ocean's damp this midnight,
the waves full of quarters I catch both hands,
bronze medallions and thin gold chains
I loop around my neck, anointing this self.

LITERATURE

What no one wants to read once out of school.
Outrages the PTA with dirty words.
Hardly ever sells at truck stops.
Makes no one rich until they're dead.
Movies never do it justice,
but every actor boasts he's steeped in it.

Outrages the PTA with dirty words,
sordid scenes of indecipherable sex.
Makes no one rich until they're dead,
and even then, no one comprehends it,
but every actress swears she's steeped in it,
at least the versions found on tape.

Despite the claim it's good for you, it's
what no one wants to read once out of school.
Rarely does it come with pictures;
hardly ever sells at truck stops.
No matter how gorgeous the film,
movies never do it justice,

but every actor boasts he's steeped in it,
novels tucked between his piled-up scripts.
Makes no one rich until they're dead,
kaput from drink or violence that
outrages the PTA with dirty words
and bloody sheets, those consequences

of thinking too much about language.
Movies never do it justice,
decent citizens boycott it.
Hardly ever sells at truck stops;
smuggled across borders in translation.
What no one wants to read once out of school.

AT SEVENTEEN I LEARNED THE TRUTH

Once I was parchment-thin, vellum-slender,
bones sharp as razors slicing soap.
Sandpaper skin, truculent armpits, tarpaper breath,
I tried to tame them with Avon creams, Love's
Baby Soft perfume, Certs stinging my tongue sweet.
But self-beautification wasn't easy in the Bronx;
I wasn't the Brooke Shields of Screvin Avenue.
Actually, I was fat, no teenaged hottie,
flab making me school's smartest girl.
Shake, shake, shake, shake your booty—
the constant drip of disco music weighed
on me, heavy as a cut, stoppered.
I couldn't dance them, but could fly,
but only when Allie let herself forget her weight.
I will rise in language, sing my caustic song.
Fat self and thin self will merge.
Mama said *una boca grande* would be
the death of me, the frown of fake designer
jeans tight across my knobby knees, chubby thighs.

MANUFACTURE

I heard today on CNN that Barbie dolls once
were made from a chemical now found to be toxic.

Imagine: blonde dolls with pink-tipped smiles
emitting lethal rays that brainwash girls

into believing bikinis are good, math too hard,
sliced bread Western civilization's pinnacle.

And supermodels—I bet they too emit
poison, bending brain waves in their

miniskirts and legwarmers, their idea of girl power
freedom from stretch marks and Freudian slips.

I bet everything in this world is slowly
poisoning us—TV sets made from nuclear waste,

credits cards, V-chips, microwaves damaging brain cells
each time I reheat another chicken pot pie. It's all

eventually genocide, isn't it—all the Prozac
and waterbeds, all the luncheon meat?

I don't know, but I remember my Barbie doll
was made of such hard plastic that I could kill

any disagreeable playmate just by smacking her
upside the head with America's favorite fashion doll.

COLLISION

You're the slinky shoe I yearn to wear,
a violin so rare it's not been made.
You're bee sting and precious honey,
purple bruise and radio static.
You're a broken vial of pheromones
spilled on my velvet kitchen floor.
For you, I'm Pavlov's dog, barking
and twitching in a Moscow kennel.
You're salt and vinegar, chips
I can't stop munching even though
I know carrots are better for my figure,
my eyes. You bring the noise, the funk,
the juice, make me quiver with a shiver
of your tongue. If you're a god,
then I can't sin. One monkey don't
stop no show, but the hard elbow
of lust can sure stop me, wake me
from slumber like a melody crooned
by witches. For you, I'm naked
in Trafalgar Square, little Miss
Goody Two-Shoes bare for her man.
And joy will thrive in sinew and eardrum.
You sexy confection, you make me
relive heaven. Take me slowly,
then *allegro, allegro*, make the roots
of dahlias quake. Shattered, you're all
over me, and I don't mind the fracture.

ALOUD

You read a poem once, it disappears.
You read a poem twice and parts
begin to stay: a phrase, a sigh, a bit
of language you might never hear again,
new words you won't encounter anywhere
except within one book that's claiming you,
asserting primacy within your brain.
Let syllables resound inside your mouth;
let lines expand to wipe out other talk:
the shrill routines of businessmen at lunch,
the gossip in the cafeteria.
You read a poem not just to understand,
but more to let its language overwhelm
your breath, to let new words in air proclaim
their pulse, a beat that ravishes and soothes
at once. So read these words aloud until
some rigid part of you goes loose—your throat,
your hands, your spine, your stupid dignity.
Read until your midnight disappears.

EROS

Desire is a song my body sings,
a bright refrain unwinding through my mind.
Deep within my cells desire rings,
leaves every wrinkle satisfied and kind.

The fact that it's my body that you want
leaves every wrinkle satisfied and kind.
Your tongue in me is such a joyous taunt,
deep within my cells desire rings.

Your kiss—it leaves me gasping here for air.
Deep within my cells desire rings—
your mouth, my skin—we pare away despair,
a bright refrain unwinding through my mind.

This pleasure leaves me shivering in sighs,
a bright refrain unwinding through my mind.
Your tongue reveals the depths between my thighs.
Desire is a song my body sings.

GRIEF: A COMPLAINT

I hate its dirty work—messy with tears,
sweat, mucus, eye-crust—hate that dry
tight feeling your chest gets while you sob,
hate the morning-after hangover-headache
after sobbing's ceased: face aching, scalp tight.
I hate the scent of flowers in a dusty
funeral home, hate the dithering over
what to wear—black skirt, black dress,
black pants. I hate chit-chat, forced smiles
turning up your mouth's corners as if
you are happy, as if all the hugging
and handshaking and back-patting
will do anyone any good. I hate
the concerned relatives who deign
to offer comfort, the family friends
who want to know what you'll do
with the house, cars, silver, furniture,
never once asking how you'll pay
the bills, parking tickets, back taxes.
I hate the bitter commerce of funerals
and cemeteries—rituals of burials
and rites of remembrance
that I want to forget as soon as they
are over, casket lowered slowly
into its trench, my heels sinking into
the just-turned mud of recent departures.

GRIEF: A PETITION

I want to limit grief to fourteen lines,
to capture it inside a rhyming box
that I can put together, then unlock
when brave enough to claim the grief that's mine.
I want to make my sorrows small enough
that I can carry them one at a time,
assured I've made a space where they're confined,
grief unrestrained too fertile, too vast and rough
to go unchecked. I need to break it down,
go bit by bit until I've built a space
with boundaries that wrap their way around,
like vines around a stake. I want grief bound,
hemmed in by words so I don't have to face
its clamoring, that unrestricted sound.

DEAD MOTHERS

They don't let go of us because they're dead;
nor can we let them go. All they have
is us—our hazy minds, our memories
revising how they spoke and walked,
what they wore, who they'd nag, ignore.

All they have is what we knew of them:
what they wore, who'd they'd nag, ignore.
We fail them every day that we're alive,
revising how they spoke and walked
us cross the street—the fingers' grip, the palm,

the cautionary voice of *no* and *stop*
that tugged us back and out of traffic's harm.
Revising how they spoke and walked,
we get their gestures wrong. The fault's in us,
is us—our hazy minds, our memories,

our mouths misquoting them. What's left
is us—our hazy minds, our memories,
our hands that cannot recreate their hands.
Nor can we let them go—all we have
bound up with how they left

and why, where they breathed their last—
hospital or desk or twisted car.
Nor can we let them go—all they have
and were remains in us, transformed or not.
They don't let go of us because they're dead.

PLAINT

Death's nomenclature? Pure trickery,
turning truths we mouth to lies.
How inaccurate to say "my late mother"
or "my late father," as if Mom's delayed

at the office, or Dad's pulling double shifts.
We say "it was her time," as if some cosmic
time clock exists, humans punching out
like assembly line workers laid off at last.

We query the widowed, the orphaned,
ask, "how are you handling it?" as if
death were clay to be shaped into some
durable object—a pitcher, a pot, an urn.

And we are such poor liars, saying
death becomes her when we mean
she doesn't look as bad as I thought
she would, claiming *it was an easy death*

when we're thinking *as breath left*
his body for good, I didn't squirm.
We watch movies where the dead
rise, and we're thrilled by terror,

ghosts so commonplace we don't gasp.
But down deep we know we still
fear bodies that do not move,
chests that will no longer swell.

We don't want to wake, partners beside us
not stirring, not moving, but sleeping like
the dead, like corpses jettisoned overboard,
sinking to depths we can't fathom.

HER WANT

What did my mother want to be,
wife to a man who'd randomly
strike out at her, then kiss her face?
Did she retreat to her mind's space
when he would yell, then laugh in glee?

What did she think of history?
What painful visions did she flee
when cancer took her to a wretched place?
What did my mother want?

Her hopes and thoughts—a mystery
I'm left with only pieces of. I see
her rise in memory, embrace
what's left, each bit and trace.
I'd wanted her to stay, for me.
What did my mother want?

ANOTHER CHILDHOOD

Our kitchen smelled from frying fish.
My mother wore her nursing shoes.
My father made my sister wish
she could escape our house, his rules.

My mother wore her nursing shoes.
My sister turned her music up—
she could escape our house, his rules
that way. I dropped another cup.

My sister turned her music up.
My father yelled at her to shut it off
right now. I dropped another cup.
You clumsy child, my father scoffed.

My father yelled at her to shut if off.
My mother told him not to shout so loud.
You nosy wife, my father scoffed.
My mother lived mild, my father proud.

My mother told him not to shout so loud.
He'd raise his fist at her, he'd threaten wrath.
My mother lived mild, my father proud.
I'd struggle with my homework, hating math.

My father called us worthless, stupid girls.
My father made my sister wish
for college far away, another world.
Our kitchen smelled from frying fish.

AWAKENING

Skin longs to be touched by your own hands—
breasts paler than the rest of you,
legs with their scars or bruises,
hair a soft down or sparse moss.
Eyes have learned to avoid

eyes, to not look further than surface of
skin, accepting what's supposed to be there:
hair, mussed before combing,
breasts unbound by underwire,
legs bare in early morning sun,

legs you usually hide from
eyes you fear will judge your body—
breasts too large or small,
skin too oily or dry,
hair too coarse or too thin.

Hair is only hair, not power.
Legs can propel you where you want;
skin is what you must learn to thrive in.
Eyes close as you touch yourself;
breasts startle beneath your fingers,

breasts no longer dormant in your hands.
Hair can wait to be washed, combed.
Eyes can stay sleep-filled.
Legs part for fingers that skim
skin that's flushing with energy—

skin warm, legs rising, eyes shut. Hair and breasts damp.

INSURRECTION

All the slaves within you
are planning to rebel—
tired of your psyche,
its thorny brand of hell.

They're planning to rebel
from what you've made them carry:
the lies you've deigned to tell,
your undetected fury.

From what you've made them carry,
their backs are bent, bruised blue,
your detected fury
set loose inside of you.

Their backs are bent, bruised blue,
their lacerations weep.
Set loose inside of you,
there's no way you can sleep.

Their lacerations weep,
tired of your psyche.
There's no way they can sleep—
all the slaves within you.

after Thomas Lux

FASHION AND BEAUTY FORECAST

Electric hair girdles.
Simulated pregnancy scars.
Creosote bleaching creams,
glass sliver nail polish.
Gasoline douches.

Brillo pad cleansing lotion.
Strychnine shower gel.
Platelet rouge. In-home
liposuction manuals.
Rib-whittling dress belts.

Elbow scrapers. Knee
resurfacing loofas.
Iron filing toenail whitener.
Marble push-up brassieres.
Asphalt lipstick. Windex

hair mousse, extra strength.
Migraine miniskirts. Shock
therapy acne treatments.
Starvation-diet smile implants.
One calorie soda, lactic acid flavor.

Calf removal surgery. Hymen
patch kit, needle included.

RECOMMENDATION LETTER

I'm writing on behalf of someone else.
I knew him in a life that's years ago.
He's just the one you want to hire.
Please give his application full attention.

I knew him in a life that's years ago,
and everything about him's faded now.
Please give his application full attention
because I tell you to, because I wrote this down

and everything about him's faded now,
except the fact that he needs a job, needs to eat.
Because I tell you to, because I wrote this down,
please look over his stats, his credits, his bio,

the fact that he needs this job, needs to eat.
He's well-trained in his field, his work.
Please look over his stats, his credits, his bio
and choose him from the throng, touch him.

He's well-trained in his field, his work,
though I can't recall his face right now.
Choose him from the throng, touch him
with life insurance, benefits, union dues.

Though I can't recall his face right now,
he's just the one you want to hire,
with life insurance, benefits, union dues.
I'm writing on behalf of someone else.

GLASSES AND BRACES

Remember that era when your feet felt so big
you swore they were boats, huge boats with clumsy
paddles? Remember braces, those cages cemented
onto your teeth, elaborate wiring jutting against

the smooth pink inside of your mouth, metals twirled
tighter each time your orthodontist put his pliers in,
his hands unnaturally soft? I'm sure you recall blemishes,
how they swelled up overnight—one day, clear,

next day, damn—right under a nostril or on
the bridge of your nose, or worse, on its tip.
You tried every soap, scrub, lotion and cream
on drugstore shelves, skin parched from scrubbing:

Noxzema stinging, Cuticura drying, Clearasil cream
so blatant it announced to everyone: here it is, acne,
hormones raging on this kid's skin, unchecked.
Could glasses have felt any heavier—

red welts pressed into either side of your nose
by frames that pinched so much you "lost" them,
mother scolding *Where are your glasses?*
as she fumbled on the couch for hers.

Back then, every revenge was sweet, so you ate
what the orthodontist told you not to: candy and gum
stuck to his intricate wirework. And if you tripped
at school, breaking your glasses beyond repair, so be it.

How you loved your mother's threat: *You're so clumsy*
I shouldn't buy you another pair!, a warning you wished
she'd follow, preferring to wander through days
of double vision than to be this geek for one more day.

REGIONAL AIRPORT

As I sit in an airport without music
except for the Muzak over the speakers—
no headphones in my bag—I'm trying
to travel light in these trying times,
to make myself inconspicuous,

wanting to eat but there's no restaurant here,
nothing but stale sandwiches in the vending machine.
To make myself inconspicuous,
I grab a magazine, hide my face.
To travel light in these trying times

I leave laptop home, carry the smallest suitcase
I own, try to keep to one carry-on
to travel light in these trying times.
I sing softly to myself, scribble poems.
No headphones in my bag, I'm trying

not to breach security, resisting the urge
to jump the single baggage claim conveyor belt.
No headphones in my bag, I'm trying
to hold boredom at bay in a one-room airport.
Except for the Muzak over the speakers,

there's no culture here—no big city flash,
no finesse in a terminal with only one airline.
Except for the Muzak over the speakers,
there's hardly any noise but this pen scratching paper
as I sit and wait in an airport without music.

WHY I LOVE SLEEP

In my dreams, everyone owns and loves Joan Armatrading records,
    while Taylor Swift slaves to earn a living wage
    at a Hoboken Howard Johnson's.
In my dreams, women direct all hip-hop videos,
    no beach scenes or thongs or limousines allowed.
In my dreams, no musical artist can record a song with a dead parent.
In my dreams, actresses attend the Oscars with bedheads, wearing
    jeans and free promotional T-shirts from local car washes;
    actors wear afghans knitted for them by expert grandmas,
    everyone oohing and ahhing at especially ambitious needlework.
In my dreams, movie studio honchos pay me to watch their flicks,
    solemnly nodding when I lecture them about product placement,
    plot holes, fake accents. In my dreams, no one ever uses
    the words "boy band." Or "silicone implants." Or "calorie-free."
In my dreams, NRA stands for *never reject anyone*—fat girls chosen
    as head cheerleaders, black guys in the swimming pool,
    French women in the thrift store. In my dreams,
    Salt Lake City is as black as Harlem. In my dreams,
    people weep over Little Willie John more than Elvis,
    his version of "Fever" on every diner jukebox.
In my dreams, teenagers get jukeboxes instead of cars
    for their sixteenth birthdays. In my dreams,
    Donny Hathaway, Lorraine Hansberry, and Laura Nyro
    all collaborate on a stage musical about Sally Hemmings
    without Jefferson. In my dreams, women host game shows,
    astronauts cook gourmet dinners for their earthbound wives.
In my dreams, chocolate is always spiked with vodka.
In my dreams, Anna Deavere Smith is president,
    striding through the White House in a crimson pantsuit so fierce
    no nation would dare instigate war—their elected officials fearing
    they could never look as sharp, speak as well, or stand as tall.

THE OLD MAN AT THE ROCK SHOW:
NEW HAVEN, CT

When Kudra starts their set, he's there, swaying
herky-jerky to the golden-haired drummer's pounding,
rushing right up to the Eddie Vedder-esque lead
singer, and we can't tell whether he wants to kick
or kiss the guy, seize his mike or pat his head.
Is he emeritus from Yale, we wonder, marveling
at his rock and roll abandon, his grasp of the
fundamental clichés: at one point, stripped
to sleeveless undershirt, he lights up matches,
stands stock still in front of the band,
saluting them with flame, one pale scrawny arm
held straight out from his body. He keeps on
twisting—one really couldn't call this dancing—
all through their set, lying down on the floor
to twitch, running from one end of the dark
boxy club to the other, a one-man mosh pit,
the floor all his. And when Sterves of Neil,
bedecked in Roy Rogers restaurant shirts,
takes the stage—what there is of it in this room
done up in post-industrial splendor, broken TVs,
buzzing with static, stuck in the wall behind
the bar—he's even more thrilled; they're louder,
faster, with bigger amps, more aggressive on
bass and guitar, lyrics crashing out of the lead
singer in pure anarchic fervor. Our guy's in heaven,
nodding his white-haired head, prancing,
loving the music the way you'd expect someone
his age to love Mozart or Cole Porter,
wizened face in ecstasy, wrinkled body

caught in its own shivery joy. When the show's
over, we wonder where he'll go—nursing home,
flophouse, grandson's basement? And will he
shake and shudder in such joy there,
more vibrant than anyone ever had a right
to suspect, naked arms thin, but hardly frail?

WATCHING *THE OMEN III: THE FINAL CONFLICT* ON LATE NIGHT CABLE

When the devil's son comes back adult, he comes back as Sam Neill
in his first American film role, long before dinos chased him
through leafy Jurassic Park. Young, he bears a disconcerting resemblance
to the singer Peter Gabriel, so much so I expect him to break into

"Shock the Monkey" at any moment. He's Damien Thorne, all
grown-up and evil, head of a conglomerate like Ted Turner's,
but without all the sports. He wears stiff suits, his hair's parted
funny, and his speaking voice is neither British nor Australian,

nowhere near as seductive as the devil's son should sound.
I never saw this '80s relic before, so I can only surmise
why the devil's son was so popular, perhaps some sort
of post-Nixon obsession with evil made obvious.

The biggest disappointment is that Satan's son is so
boring, even as he plots to kill all the baby boys born
on March 24, date of Jesus's second coming. Funny,
I thought he'd reappear in December, bearing party favors.

Meanwhile there's some silliness with knife-bearing
Italian monks who've come to kill Thorne, wind up
dead themselves. I can't figure out why Thorne
has so many minions—his devilish plans are no fun,

and they don't involve chocolate, dancing, or heavy
metal music. Neill plays him like he's the loneliest guy
on earth, and before the last monk standing has his
showdown with Satan's scion, I've fallen asleep,

bored by his precise dullness, his lack of sartorial
splendor, his whining that humans love Jesus more.
Of course we do. Jesus has wicked fashion sense,
great hair, and a flair for suppers that last.

JAYNE WITH A "Y"

for Jayne Mansfield

Queen of the Chihuahua Show, Queen of the Palm
Springs Rodeo, your aliases grew like your bust:
Miss Tomato, Miss Lobster, Queen of
Refrigeration Week, Miss Direct Mail.
Your heart-shaped life had a heart-shaped bed;
you bathed in pink bubbles in a heart-shaped tub,
pink champagne spurting from a marble fountain
in your Pink Palace on Sunset Boulevard.
46-24-36, you wobbled down the street
in *The Girl Can't Help It*, men's eyeglasses
shattering at the sight of you, your teeter-
totter mincing walk, your swiveling hips.
Playboy's Valentine Playmate from '55
to '58, your 168 IQ let you know breasts
were your ticket out of Texas, and if
they happened to come loose from whatever
you wore, that could only help you upstage
that other Jane, Howard Hughes's toy.
Who else could you marry but Mr. Universe,
the only man with a chest bigger than yours?

But 1958 turned 1966, and bosoms went
flat, movie stars turned Mia Farrow-pixyish.
No one wanted to see your tipsy strut except
drag queens who primped versions of you
in a look-alike contest only you could judge.
1967, June, 2:25 a.m., and your silver
Buick collided with a truck in the fog,
your children safely sleeping in the back,
your Chihuahua dead in your arms.

CHASING MARIAN

Would you think I was crazy
if I told you the sexiest scene in movies
occurs in *The Music Man*, when Robert Preston,
as Prof. Harold Hill, chases Shirley Jones' Marian,
all around the town's library, pursuing her
though the patrons continually shush him,
trying to quiet his passion? You know
the plot: Hill comes to town,
promising the citizens brass band instruments—
Seventy-six trombones and a dream of happy parents,
beaming kids. But in this scene,
all he's after is Marian, in her strait-laced
spinster librarian's blouse, every bit of ardor
buttoned in, tamped down as she flits
through the library, stacking books, shelving passion.
But Hill, through song, wins the patrons over,
until one by one, they're dancing, turning
somersaults, men whirling women
around and between tables and chairs,
books threatening to cascade around them,
fall from the stacks she's so neatly made.
But this being a musical, Hill
doesn't get her yet—she's still resistant,
fettered by tight convention,
a finger to her lips to hush what's stirring
beneath. But if Hill wanted to pursue me
in a library, I'd be game, buttons
on my high-necked blouse popping off
one by one, his serenade going straight
to my head, my lips unpursed, skirt unzipped.

MS. JACKSON REPLIES

after "Ms. Jackson," by OutKast

You never meant to make my daughter cry,
but you did. She's wasted too many hours moaning,
sobbing about you and this baby-child, the way

you never come to visit. She blames me for keeping
you away, claims I said you're worthless, shiftless.
I never said no such thing, just that my girl deserves

better than you—with your rapping and jiving,
your music career. I say a career means a man
puts on a coat and tie, speaks correct, knows

English the way it's supposed to be spoken,
not hopping around on stage like someone
on fire. I don't need a roughneck teaching

my grandchild to cuss and drink, to stay up
all hours of the night making music
while respectable men sleep. What kind

of music is that noise anyway—all that silly
rhyming no one can make sense of, just
an excuse for filthy language and a loud beat.

Now if my girl's baby was by Wynton Marsalis,
I wouldn't have a problem—such a fine young
man from a good family with a good education,

so smart they had him on public television
all month. But you, you get on TV and embarrass
me with your so-called apology, saying *you're sorry*

a trillion times. You don't even know
how to count, much less how much
a trillion is. You say you're for real,

but all I see is a phony who raps about hoes
while his child grows up without a proper
role model. You say you're sorry, but not

as sorry as I am that I didn't stop you
from ever seeing, much less touching, my daughter.
You work my last nerve, my last bit of patience,

and I'm not too old to take my belt to you,
let you know how Ms. Jackson gets business done.
But I'm a lady, won't sink to your level.

Just keep sending money, but stay away—
my daughter none of your concern, this
grandchild more like me than you will ever know.

THE WORLD'S WORST WHITE SUPREMACIST

He's got acne, needs a personal trainer,
has mousy brown hair with unruly waves.
He stutters, and it's embarrassing to stutter

when he has to say "white power" over
and over—all those w's. Spindly, sunken-
chested, sharp-nosed and sweaty, does he

come from good stock? Questionable.
A stint in boot camp would kill him—
if not the exercise, then the integration.

Black people giggle when he walks by,
hardly fearing this architect of today's
racial hatreds, not scary like Metzger

or sly like Duke. He leaves the mayhem
to his devotees, knowing bloody hands
will sully his cause, make him less foxy

to all those white-supremacist-loving females
out there. He favors polyester, plays a mean
violin, though the orchestra fired him

when they saw that video of him
using the Israeli flag for a floor mat.
He's suing them, and the state, and

you, too, okay—if you violate
his copyright. You see, he's a lawyer,
and if there's anything people like less

than a lawyer, it's a white supremacist
lawyer, especially one that stutters
and swears, litigates and instigates.

RUINED THINGS

Growing up, I learned to see ruined things as normal,
almost beautiful: rusted cars forsaken in driveways,

faded awnings flapping loose over two-story brick
storefronts, letters in neon signs flickering, burning

out. I learned to follow the ecstatic swirls and curves
of graffiti on walls, loving the mutant alphabet

sprayed on by street artists, letters swollen as clouds,
puffy hieroglyphs. And every empty lot was strewn

with what people has failed to take with them,
dumped, I thought, for me to explore, poke

with a sharp, whittled stick: shreds of skin mags
torn in the underbrush, clothes ripped to rags

snagged among tree branches, blown tires
and dented hubcaps spread out like a welcome

in my neighborhood's arid patches,
Bronx land the city left unclaimed.

Nothing wrong in being worn, eroded under
urban sun and soot, colors muted in subway

stops, bus stations, dirt and rust and wear
all honorable to me, every new building sagging

eventually, every new school soon marked
by any and every color that could be sprayed on.

Nothing left pristine in that city-scape I loved,
nothing clean or clean in all I remember—lives

punctuated by the jagged symmetry
of wrecked windows, broken barbed wire.

EMERGENCY ROOMS

I know the dowdy walls of hospitals,
the scuffs from footsteps streaking tile.
I know this molded plastic chair,
dust gathering in corners, crevasses.
The white-faced clock whose hands
don't move, the rumpled magazines—
I've seen them all, anxious.

I've heard the static of TVs;
I know this molded plastic chair.
I've heard the coughs from aching chests.
The white-faced clock whose hands
slowed down can't count the nervous hours.
I've seen them all, anxious—
doctors hustling through, the nurses

weary in their drab pastels.
I've heard the coughs from aching chests,
seen drops of blood a mop did not wipe out.
Slowed down, can't count the nervous hours,
I try to rouse myself, to stay alert.
Doctors hustling through, the nurses—
no words for me, no soothing news.

Don't move the rumpled magazines.
Seen drops of blood a mop did not wipe out,
dust gathering in corners, crevasses.
I try to rouse myself, to stay alert—
I know this molded plastic chair.
No words for me, no soothing news.
I know the dowdy walls of hospitals.

RULES FOR WRITING

Never mention any bodily functions,
especially any function that produces
stains of any kind. Never make
anyone cry, or laugh, or touch them
or arouse them, eyes on your own
paper, fingers where we

can see them. Never dance, never
curse, never sing, don't rhyme—
or rather, do rhyme, but only where
and when we tell you. Stand
up straight, no slouching, no yelling,
don't wear that, wear this—

each button buttoned all the way
to the top. Don't wiggle, don't fidget,
don't leave thumbprints, handmarks,
pencil shavings, or nail clippings.
Don't chew things. Don't lie.
Don't spill anything. Sit this way,

not that way; don't do anything
you can't explain. Don't, don't,
don't, don't—do not leave this room
without inspection, without
passing this desk first—
this implacable, unfeeling desk.

THE COURTSHIP OF MISERY AND ILLNESS

Misery and illness border each other, true neighbors.
They bleed into each other until you shiver from fever

and nightmare, from waking dreams, dreamy wakes.
Misery loves how illness makes you gaunt, frantic

for medicine, for anything to restore color to your
pallor, rouse your cells to fight infection, invasion.

Illness courts misery, sends her love notes and fragrant
sachets, swoons over misery's snapshot in a gilt frame.

Misery and illness get along so well they marry,
set up housekeeping in your blood, in the tiny kingdoms

of your corpuscles, in your dermis, dentin, cilia.
Illness goes shopping, buys the groceries,

makes thin broths from gristle, saltines, porridge.
Misery decorates: garlands of wadded tissues,

unrinsed empty glasses, teaspoons coated with
cough syrup's thick resin. Misery loves illness,

even though he's a slut, a flirt who will tongue-kiss
anyone, put any lucky girl on her back, boy on his side.

And now that misery and illness have moved in,
made their home in you, pushed you down,

forced you into bed—now that they've taken over,
there's nothing left for them to do but breed,

thrive in your writhing, your breathing,
your inflamed mouth, surly eyes.

WHAT THEY'RE THINKING WHILE
YOU'RE READING YOUR POEMS

You're standing there, in your neat suit or scruffy jeans,
sheaf of new poems in your trembling hands, voice
barely audible so that the woman in the floral hat yells

louder!, and you twist the cranky microphone closer
to your mouth, yell *better, is that better?,* hope no one
will notice the shudder your voice acquires the longer

you read. A short solemn man in a tweed jacket
stares right at you, but he's really dreaming of his
bathtub, his woman, and bubbles, nothing but bubbles;

the long-legged gawky teenager who's no longer
really a teenager contemplates degrees of speed
instead of you, postulates how fast his jeep can fly

down the steepest hills in this town you've never
seen before. The couple who's so in love
with being seen beams at you, your silly lines,

but they're already way past you, smiling because
they know who'll be roleplaying "cabana boy
and kidnapped heiress" tonight, soon as this

bloody reading's over, you no longer standing there,
droning your small inevitable stories. That blonde
girl wants brownies. That math teacher in plaid

wants the blonde girl, and the math teacher's wife,
rotund and prone to gossip, wants her cell phone.
Later, each one of these people will tell you

how much they loved your poems,
especially the ones about God, that one
three letter word you never mentioned

GIVING UP WRITING

Let's face it, you don't have it
anymore, and maybe, you never
did. There's always someone
smarter than you, with better
connections, a cooler author's
photo. There's always someone
strutting about like a porn star,
jazzed about their latest—it's
the best they've ever written,
and it came so easily, dictation
sanctioned by God. There's
always someone unwrapping
the first shiny copy of a brand
new book, their name in big
letters on the spine, front cover,
all sorts of embarrassing praise
on the back. Let's face it,
you've got a few scribbled notes,
a few undisciplined lines,
and achy knees from kneeling
too much, praying the Lord
or any acceptable substitute
will make of you an instrument.
Maybe you're not fit for music,
you're thinking, with your busted
gut strings, disheveled hair. Maybe
silence is all you can handle among
the glossy and well-groomed.
Think of all the failures before you,
how they refused to let critics shut

them down. Or up. Think, and
pause before you write again,
knowing what you have to say
has nothing to do with anyone
but you. Give up writing for them,
the naysayers and doomspreaders,
and say what you need to for me,
one solitary woman waiting states
or decades or continents away,
listening for the thrum of your life.

MY MUSE

wears thigh-high black leather boots,
    sports an eight inch 'fro so thick
        she can hide razor blades in it,
fingers nimble as she slices away
    weak lines, slack syllables, unredeemed
        clichés. She smells of cocoa butter,
has skin the color of a Hershey's kiss,
    stomach firm without sit-ups. Stroking
        her sinuous waist, she dares me to write
as well as she looks, her smile more wicked
    than I could ever be. When she speaks,
        she sings; when she sings, I stop, gape
at her mouth—lips full, lightly pink;
    unlike me, she's never been ashamed
        of them, of her wide nose, hands.
She's not afraid of anything, anyone,
    but I'm afraid of her—what if I
        let her down, anger her, displease her
with gooey sentiment, abstract diction?
    Patient thus far, she marches
        down the hallway to the kitchen
to cut herself a slice of chocolate
    peanut butter pie, says I can have some
        if I get down to business, write her
something deserving such sweetness.
    She'd never be caught in polyester
        like I wore in grade school, seat
of my pants snagging on wooden chairs.
    She's a clean-up woman,
        a stand-up woman who comes

and goes as she pleases, the plate
    she holds out to me laden
        with what I want, have to earn.

MISTAKEN IDENTITY

The day I became Rita Dove in a bathroom
in a library in Harrison, Arkansas, a little
old white lady tottered up to me while I

was washing my hands to ask if I
was the Poet Laureate she'd read about
during the library's eight week "Poets

in Person" series. I wanted to say yes,
had to say no, told the tiny woman
with the fluttery hands and the parchment

skin that I hoped one day to be as good
as Rita Dove, and that, yes, I was a poet,
live and in person in her local library.

Just not that poet; just not that famous.
That day no men in white robes
stood in the center of town in Harrison,

Arkansas to declare their hatred of all
things wretched and black; that day
no rally made the evening news with

slogans and fists and wizards. That day
one small white woman, trembling with
age and astonishment, stood in awe

of one black woman, even if I wasn't
quite the poet she wanted. I can't fault her
for wanting to find a poet in the bathroom

of the library in Harrison, Arkansas,
can only thank her for having the sublime
taste to mistake me from someone more

famous and more talented when if I'd
showed up on the wrong day in Harrison,
Arkansas, I'd be tree bait—and no poem

or prayer could have helped me then,
saved me from the immaculate white men
and their history, in Harrison, in Arkansas.

SEAMSTRESS, 1946

after the painting by Jacob Lawrence

Face hidden behind ancient iron-black machine
her shoulders hunch over its whirring needle—
she feeds it red cloth   full of rectangles of flowers
red spool feeds red thread into the needle
between her articulate fingers she doesn't sing
as she works doesn't smile lips on dark brown face
don't curve no joy her dressmaker's dummies
lurk behind her green cloth strung from one to the other
is this her house her world   her factory?
How many dresses must she sew
sweating through her bright white shirt
under the light tucked into the underbelly
of this black hulk she operates one palm on its wheel
other guiding fabric? Does she sew because she wants to
because she has to no makeup no polish
on her long brown fingers head scarf over her hair
black as this anvil that makes seams   she is a collage
of labor   she is pigment   paint on solitary paper.

LOOKING IS FOR POETS

so is staring, peering, inspecting your life
with a glare so keen you flinch—fearful
of these people called poets—liars spouting
fancy words and metaphors, language
that's never just language, always something
more behind the letters. You wish they'd
stop examining, prodding, hoping to find
some fact you don't even know yourself,
a secret so buried you never speak of it—
the scars, burns, and shame too deep.
At first, you thought poets entertaining—
their rhythms and postures, eagerness
to please with rhyme and color. But then
they started to get beneath your skin,
provoking questions about your childhood,
your sleepwalking, your glass of wine
at bedtime, your fistful of pills come morn.
All these poets—the dead and the live ones,
the black and brown and white ones,
the male and female ones—you fear
they'll make you as neurotic as they are,
haunted by double meanings, phrases,
intimations of mortality. So you pick up
the anthology, wave it over the trash can,
but the words, the words, the words keep
stopping you—*because I could not stop for death*—
I have wasted my life—*we die soon*—
and you can't throw all that looking
away, all those caustic, crucial visions.

FIGURE STUDY, RECLINING FEMALE

You make me the object of your gaze,
etch me in strokes on paper, my likeness
a haunted chiaroscuro, my wary face

turned out to meet your viewer, naked
body turned for privacy, the bedspread—
our bedspread—rumpled and gathered

below my feet, tossed there as if after
consummation. I sling one arm across
my breasts, elbow out, look over my

shoulder, do not smile because a smile
will ruin this, your reckoning of me.
Instead you detail my hair, eyes,

heels, the small of my back, curves,
the bare plain terrain of my stomach.
Here our bed is documented for your

public: our pillow and mattress
slung on the floor, our walls unadorned.
You claim you adore me, that I must

stay still, pose glacial and transparent
for an etching that will hang in a gallery
hours and years from your barren studio.

Why do you not paint me with color,
make me vibrate instead of shiver,
my skin flushed pink as it actually is?

No one will know me except for this
facade, and those who see this portrait
will think me passive, submissive, far

from feminist. But to know all I am
will take more pictures than you can create,
will take a finer artist to make me live.

MEA CULPA

Before this poem even begins, let me
apologize—I was drunk or high or
lovesick when I wrote it, and I knew

right away it wasn't going to work.
I'm already at line five, and I haven't
even used a single poetic device—

not a simile, not a metaphor, no paradoxes
or oxymorons. That's what I feel like
half the time, a moron, poet spilling details

to strangers, hoping someone will listen,
pronounce it good, profound. Instead
of this mad scribbling, this imperfect wail,

I could go do something useful: para-
sailing or morel hunting, hear something
other than my own moody warbling.

Look, I'm really sorry, this didn't turn out
like I planned—I was going to have you
walk away from this poem misty-eyed,

yet impressed with my wit, my diction.
But this poem is bald and toothless, whiny,
gutless, eager to please. So I say mea culpa,

please forgive me, assess no penalty
on a poet who's only trying her best,
hands and brain disconnected, voice

audible only to her own crooked ear.

PHILOLOGIST

The Grammar Lady wants to lay you down,
sink you in her cushy canopy bed,
pausing then to look straight down at you,
before she lies with you in lacy sheets.

She whispers as she's making love to you
that split infinitives make her so mad
she'd rather spit than boldly go where no
grammar hotline specialist has gone,

her breasts both sensuous and sensual,
a Botticelli woman trapped inside
her bargain basement suits. Within her bed,
you are a celebrant, more than a reveler

or party guest; her body is a ceremony
that both surprises and astonishes;
she's ravishing, but never ravage her.
She's vulnerable, but not susceptible

to gentlemen deceiving her in bed,
voluptuous between these folds of silk.
You're her voluptuary here, indulging
in her smarts, her skin, her scent—

her luxuriant hair unspooling in this
luxurious bed—feather pillows, goose down
comforter. Ardor isn't rigorous for her,
her passions hardly difficult—this bed,

your touch, precision in the words she says
and writes. You'll set her swooning if you know
your clinch tonight is more than just a clench.
Embracing her, you learn to be discreet,

but not discrete, not separate when she
makes her effect, affecting you in ways
mere words cannot contain, the change
she starts in you blatant, but never flagrant.

CHALAZION

Such a funny word
for such a little thing,
a blister on the edge
the eyelid pulls over the cornea,
the thin rim we never think of
until the chalazion lodges there,
big as a boulder, small as a drop.
I seem to get one every
ten years, so every ten years
a surgeon's disciplined tools
scrape away this bit of flesh,
sealing the wound with lasers,
so I can blink again without
feeling as if my eyeball's
been scratched by a fingernail.
I walk around for half a day
with gauze swaddling my bandaged
eye, medicinal drops stinging
infection away. And I remember
the lump the surgeon showed me,
pea-sized, undistinguished flesh
gone wrong, a growth to mark
the decade's flaws, let me know
how the body can go astray
in smallest, quietest ways.

FUNK BOX

for Jon

You make me want music in the morning
bumping funk to go along with my ham and eggs
high hat and snare drum thump
way before noon when virtuous people
are asleep or getting ready for work

way before noon when virtuous people
are too busy to swivel their hips
in gratitude for what God gave them
whatever shape God comes in:
bumping funk to go along with my ham and eggs,

high hat and snare drum, thump
that's syncopated enough to get
my body moving, my mouth working
wrapping its way around a song's
high hat and snare drum thump.

Bumping funk to go along with my ham and eggs,
you smile your little wicked smile,
that I could care less what the neighbors think grin.
So what if you're playing Bootsy and P-Funk
way before noon when virtuous people

are asleep or getting ready for work,
not studying funk beats and the moments
between them, whatever can echo before and after,
those fine distinctions between getting up and getting down.
You make me want music in the morning.

ODE TO MY STOMACH

My, you are persistent—
no matter the diet,
the exercise—sit-ups,
knee lifts—you still
carry this flesh I am
supposed to dislike,
to whittle away until
the muscles there
lie flat and sculpted,
a six-pack, hard enough
to take a punch.
When I close my jeans,
the little metal button
imprints itself on you,
trying to rein you in,
make you stay within
boundaries of denim
and stitching. You
could grow and grow
until you hang down
past my knees, and I
would have to gather
you in my hands, shove
you back in place.
You want to be wide,
to spread, to rise
like yeasty bread I
cannot resist—you
make me unpretty
to others, you make me

glad when I curl into myself
to sleep, a soft swelling
warm in my hands
as a baby, the baby
that would make this stomach
even wider, even less pretty.
My tummy, my fat, my excess,
I stroke lotion over you,
skin under my fingertips,
flesh under my fingertips.
You might outlive me—
belly in the afterlife, bulge in the beyond.

ORDINARY DRESS

I never cared for wedding gowns.
Got married in purple and black,
a dress with black buttons up and down—
it hangs in my closet still, stuck in the back.

Got married in purple with a black
collar, long sleeves, hem right at my knee.
It hangs in my closet still, stuck in the back—
it's too tight now, too small for me.

Collar, long sleeves, hem at my knee,
cloth too thin for Indiana winter, December.
It's too tight now, too small for me,
all I can do is remember—

cloth too thin for Indiana winter, December.
Wind whipped it open. I had to pin it shut.
All I can do is remember
my sheer stockings and my trembling.

When wind whipped it open, I had to pin it shut
with a borrowed safety pin.
My sheer stockings and my trembling
made no difference to my future husband.

Held together with a borrowed safety pin,
I said vows I've since forgotten.
Made no difference to my husband,
who cares little about how fat I've gotten.

I said vows I've since forgotten,
keep a dress with black buttons up and down.
Don't care about how fat I've gotten.
I'll never wear a wedding gown.

LOVE POEM

Your body knows the history of mine:
you've stroked my hair, my face, my cheeks,
a wrinkle that was once a tiny line,
a bicep muscle gone from strong to weak.

Your fingers know my curves and bones;
you've kissed the scars that will not fade.
No matter that my waist has grown;
through gain and loss, you always stayed.

This bicep muscle's gone from strong to weak.
Through gain and loss, you always stayed
to comfort me if I don't want to speak,
confused about the choices I have made.

You look at me as if I'm still as fine,
as taut. You pledge that I won't be alone,
no matter what my shape, changing design.
The body you embrace I won't disown.

You've stroked my hair, my face, my cheek;
you've kissed the scars that will not fade.
So what if I'm no longer sleek—
my body's one I wouldn't trade.

Your body knows the history of mine,
your fingers know my curves and bones.
You look at me as if I'm still as fine,
as taut. You pledge that I won't be alone.

TOKEN BLACK

Somehow you thought enough of me
to let me in this classroom, as long
as I sit quietly, not uttering a word.

Somehow you thought that I could be
brought up to speed, made to obey,
made to read history the way

you want me to: no blame for anyone,
no fingerpointing, no blood. That's what
you think I'm here to do: smile

and nod in gratitude for the chance
I've been given to learn about this
great nation from texts that don't mention

anything black that isn't followed
by the words "poverty" or "underclass."
You've no idea what's happening in the hollows

of my body: my stomach, my fists;
no idea of the taste of bile behind
my lips, back of my throat. You see a smile,

a laugh you cannot hear the mockery in.
For who can doubt your graciousness?
You've let me in, offered me a chair,

a glimpse of the knowledge I can win,
as long as I sit behind this marred desk—
my face quiet, mouth a wooden slit.

RADIOS

I had one in the shape of a Sunoco gas pump,
static crackling through its tiny speaker,
station numbers popping up in small windows
as if to ring up a full tank sale. I had one
that sat on the corner of my desk through
junior high, black box of AM and FM,
shaky particleboard desk wobbling under
the weight of textbooks, of vibrations I'd
make more intense by putting my hand
on the spindly antenna, coaxing more music
into the air, my body a conduit for sounds
from someplace else, my first "turn that
down or I'll take it away" radio, my father
regretting he ever taught me to love music.
I had a silver boom box, so fancy with its
tape deck and knobs for bass and treble,
signal light gleaming red to show a station's
location, a secret plucked from the airwaves.
I had double tape decks, alarm clock radios,
portable cassette players so I could pump
the music right into my skull, ignore
the chatter of voices unaccompanied by melody.

Now, I own too many radios, but I don't
listen to the radio, no call letters burned
into my brain, no numbers once more familiar
than my locker combination. Now we only
listen to the radio locked into the dark
of our car as we creep past Memphis—
old school-love ballads making the night

that much more lush, marriage more
than the daily repetitions our bodies know—
eating, bathing, rinsing dishes. Husband
and wife, we croon along until the signal fades,
the music's gone, and we're silent, hungry.

SIDEKICKS

In the movies, they're the dependable ones—
cast to make the male lead more macho,
the female more attractive, thinner. But they
get the best lines, wisecracks and comebacks
everyone leaves the theater quoting. In
romantic comedies, the sidekicks are friendly

advice-givers, there to soothe Jennifer Aniston
or Lawrence with a box of tissues and a
pint of rocky road when they can't figure out
the obvious about their airbrushed love lives,
though we in the audience knows Jennifers
will always end up with whatever man

they want, their ever-faithful friends content
to pick out bridesmaid's dresses. In action
flicks, the sidekick's often the comic relief,
the bug-eyed black guy who gives our hero
vital information when he should be saving
his own skin, leaving Brad—Cooper or Pitt—

to suffer whatever fate should befall them—
bomb plots, nuclear threats. No one becomes
an actor to play the sidekick, to be the one
sitting home Saturday night so the star can call
with romantic details, the one inventing alibis
for the cop gone AWOL, lawyer gone nuts.

For once, I want a movie where all the sidekicks
shout *no, I'm not going to help you get the girl*
or save the world or win your stupid lawsuit,
a picture where the comic relief refuses
to spout funny lines during car chases, prison
breaks. Just once, I want to pay my $10.50 to see

a film where the chubby confidant and the black
guy run off together, get a motel room with a
vibrating bed, an endless supply of quarters,
all Jennifers and Brads abandoned,
left to solve the plot themselves, no more advice
from actors who always get second billing.

Deleted. Remaindered.
Reduced for quick sale.
Shoved in the bargain bin.
Discounted, then destroyed.
Pulped. Torched. Shredded.
Marked down, written off,
sold to the lowest bidder.
Can't give it away. No takers.
Finders, no keepers.
Bundle it with the trash.
Put it where the dogs
can find it, leave it for
the garbage collectors,
scavengers, Salvation Army bins
and thrift shop counters.
Slip it under the cat's dish,
let it line closets you no longer
use. Drop it off in back
of the local bordello,
let the clientele dirty it
with covert footsteps.
Run it up a flagpole,
see if anyone salutes.
Out of sight, out of mind,
out of reach, out of touch.
Just lift your arms
above your head
—like the cop says—
walk away and no one
will get hurt.

KEISHA ADDRESSES HER TEACHER
ON THE ART OF POETRY

Just a bunch of pretty lies white people tell, then
test you on it, claim you don't get it 'cause you're
culturally deprived. What they really mean is
depraved—my people too violent, too subhuman

to understand. The poems my teacher likes
have no ribs in them, no greens, no taste
or grease or salt, and I'm just not feeling them,
so I don't say nothing, sit in the back of the room

so she won't point her bony finger, ask me
to analyze these poems she loves so much.
Just words that make no kind of sense, written
in lines to fool me. She wants to call me

ignorant, tell me I'm wrong when I say I don't
see nothing in her white woman's poetry.
She wants me to read from this book with all
print and no pictures, questions after each poem

that I can't answer. White lady, I want you to listen
to *this* poem. Keisha got something to say that
ain't in your damn books, your silly-ass stories.
My poem's got big lips, juicy ones that suck and kiss.

My poem's got hips, no sorry sack of scrawny. My poem
don't make nobody yawn, like yours do. My poem
can wake all the people you've put to sleep all these years,
make them rise again to dance before their bones die.

PIPPI LONGSTOCKING

Ugly as someone's snotty kid brother, you're
as red-headed as a hound, as a scratched sore.
So what if you're the strongest girl in the world?
Your braids stick out like the tail on a pig,
like someone wrapped your hair around wire,
your elbows bony and sooty, scabby as
alligator skin. Freckled as a moon, you
never bathe, skinny and raw-boned as a starved
cowboy. Why do you get to live in a house
with no parents, no rules, no adults telling
you what to do, a monkey and a horse
for your counsel? Talky as a sportscaster,
you'd lift anything above your head—carts,
boats, me—anything to prove your super-girl
strength. You'd talk and talk until the sun
went down—crazy shoeless girl abandoned
by your vagrant seafaring father. No school for you,
no library or orphanage. You should be lonely
as a book no one checks out, but you live
the life I want—no rules but the ones you make,
no grades needed to show the world you're smart.

PEOPLE: A BALLADE

They fuck things up, they get facts wrong,
they mispronounce your name, despite correction.
They overlook your paintings, verse, or song,
then wonder why you're given to dejection.
They stare at you, locating imperfections,
find every fault you have, without and within.
They'll gossip at your slightest indiscretion.
People disappoint you again and again,

abandon you when nights grow long.
When hard work requires determination,
only a few will remain from the initial throng
that promised aid and cash. The rest are on vacation,
not answering their phones. Rejection
makes the world go round, that spin
of abandonment, of least protection.
People disappoint you again and again,

failing to come through, implying you don't belong,
ignoring your efforts with no inspection
of what you have produced. Can you stay strong
when no one shows for your production
of *Candide*, your slide show, your investigation
into 18th century mores? Can you deal if fewer than ten
show to hear you, say two? Despite finest intentions,
people disappoint you again and again.

Friends, don't create expecting approbation;
big crowds will only cheer you if you win,
and only until some other provocation.
People disappoint you again and again.

LAUREATE

He might say something wise enough to print.
She might make poetry more popular
than shin splints or those globs of pocket lint
inside your washed-out jeans. He might just bore
assemblies of the first- or seventh-grades;
she might disrobe and leave us all in shock.
He might not want to be here, but you paid
for all his expertise, his wit, his stock
responses to the questions asked each time:
Why write? Why poetry, why not real books?
Can what you've read be poetry, sans rhyme?
She might be thinking of her faded looks—
her sad visage poetic, but not for words.
He might be drunk right now, all vision blurred.

WHY I'M A TERRIBLE BED
AND BREAKFAST PATRON

I'm always afraid I'll break the antiques,
and frankly, I don't really care for them,
one chair as good as another to me—
as long as it accommodates my butt.
I don't like innkeeper small talk, refuse
to pet the resident dog or cat, not caring
how old the house is, or who owned it
before the current owners, or where
the drapes came from or how authentically
the grounds have been restored to former
glory. Reluctant to leave a cheery message
in the guest book—isn't the fact I stayed here
enough?—I know the owners want ooohing
and aahing from me, curiosity, expressions
of awe about floral patterns and chifforobes.
I'm sorry. I can't do it. I don't care about
who slept here a hundred years ago, or twenty
years ago, or last night. I don't care how
aged the trees are out front, what flowers,
freshly cut, reside in these vases one of my
clumsy elbows might send skidding to parquet
floors. I want to go home, where the chairs
don't match, the lawn's got stumps from sawing
down trees of no historical significance,
and the carpets came from the discount place
down the highway. I want to go home
where hands that only I know will cook
my breakfast, will caress my lips and face
to welcome me home, back to my own bed.

WOMEN'S ENCOUNTER GROUP: SUNDAY FUNNIES

Casper drives me crazy with his lies,
stutters Wendy, in tears. The others nod.
Nancy's gruff, claims Sluggo never tries
to think about her needs. *He's kind of odd,*

mutters Wendy, in tears. The others nod,
take notes, intent on learning how
to think about their needs. It's kind of odd
to see them glum like this—unsmiling now,

taking notes, intent on learning how
to make relationships work. Olive Oyl reports
to see them glum like this, unsmiling now,
reminds her Popeye's late with child support.

To make relationships work, Olive Oyl reports,
you've got to let them know who's boss.
Remind her Popeye's late with child support,
Cathy sneers. Broom-Hilda wants to toss

these girls aside, let them know who's boss.
But Lucy keeps the session going, on track.
Cathy sneers, *Broom-Hilda wants to toss*
me out of here, poised to attack.

Lucy keeps the session going, on track,
her fees increasing every time. Wendy cries,
Get me out of here, poised to attack.
You've got to get a grip, Lucy sighs.

Her pleas increasing every time, Wendy cries.
Nancy's gruff, claims Sluggo never tries
to make it work. Wendy slumps, then sighs:
Casper drives me crazy with his lies.

BEAUTY QUEENS I WISH EXISTED

Let's hear it for Miss Iambic Pentameter, so shapely
and pert she's five times the woman I'll ever be.
And stepping to the stage right now is Miss
Popular despite Her Threadbare Wardrobe
and Lack of Fashion Sense—her teeth and crown
skew crooked, but everybody loves her anyway.
Mrs. Leave the Kids at Home 'Cause I Won't
Be Back Till Wednesday sends her regrets—
and her laundry. But don't worry, Miss Laundry World
has her whites and colors separated, under control;
she's spin-cycle perfection. Miss Orthopedic Shoe
no longer hobbles on her way to the mailbox,
support hose and floral duster completing
her ensemble. Perhaps she will make friends
with Miss Mall on the Bad Side of Town,
both of them sad for all the boarded-up stores.
Ms. Funeral Home Attendant, Ms. Dogcatcher,
Ms. Happy That I Don't Have to Be a Bank
Guard Anymore all pose with the most genuine
of smiles, no bikini butt tape to make them frown.
Ms. Dollar Store Cashier confers with Mrs. Pharmacy
Checkout Girl on proper register technique—
receipt and change delivered in one swift motion,
"thank you, come again" a song that's not lost
its music. Ms. Sonnet is here, Ms. Blank Verse,
and that trickster, Ms. Sestina—but no one
has seen Ms. Villanelle, despite her eager refrains.
Ms Wannabe Policewoman wants to write
a warrant for my arrest, but Ms. Plagiarism Detective
cites her for lack of originality, backed by the wiles

of America's Top Girl Computer Troubleshooter.
Ms. No-Fly Zone, Ms. Eagle Scout, Ms. Heightened
Anxieties could keep me up all night with their barking,
but Ms. World Mini Mart has everything I need:
salty snacks, cold sodas, candies I'll chew for days
so Ms. Orthodontist can undo the damage.
And please, keep Ms. One Night Stand and Mrs. Eighth-
Grade Hall Monitor apart—the man they've both
straddled is slinking out the theatre's back door
with Miss Late for Work, but So Charming
You Forgive Her and Take Her out to Lunch,
their arms entwined, her sash undone.

GIVEN NAMES

I could never be Wendy—Wendys
have pert noses, even perkier
breasts. And I don't think
I could handle being Ernestine—
that name comes with the weight
of sensible shoes, oat bran.
Because I refuse to spend more
than five dollars on a single
bottle of shampoo, I could not be
Tatiana, no silken fall of hair
to toss over one shoulder.
I could not be Marci, Cindi, or Lindi—
harbor no desire for a name
junior high girls spell with a heart,
instead of a black dot above the i.
Virtuous names resonate with goodness
I cannot live up to—too clumsy
to be Grace, too cynical to be Hope,
too stingy to be Charity. My mother
wanted to name me Maria—and I
could have lived with that—
men serenading me, singing like
eager members from a touring company
of *West Side Story*. But my father
said *no, that's a bad woman's name,*
so that life of avid crooners
was never mine. Instead, men walk up to me,
singing *Allison*—and I curse the sarcastic Brit
who wrote that song, a song where the singer
hates himself for loving a woman

like me, still claiming his aim is true
as the instrumentation fades,
though we both know it never will be.

CAMP COUNSELOR

Vacations home from college I found work
at a private summer camp for wealthy kids—
three hundred bucks a month to entertain
a bunch of nine-year-olds who'd shriek my name
as if it were a novelty. I'd leave
each evening aching from their weight—they'd pull
my arms and legs, drag me reluctantly
down halls inside the school where camp was held.
The noise that thirteen nine-year-olds could make
assured my head would throb all bus ride home.
And every kid had needs, demands to fill:
no milk for Mikey Scott, and Brittany,
allergic to the paints in arts and crafts,
could only draw with crayons thick as thumbs.
The camp director was a cheery man
who'd welcomed me on staff despite the fact
I hadn't gone to school in Riverdale,
the ritzy neighborhood that school was in.
I did my job, tried not to get attached
to kids I wouldn't ever see again,
but found myself embracing all their faults:
the boys, obsessed with air hockey contests,
the girls, who sang Madonna songs and preened.
I wondered if they knew what "virgin" meant.
They told me of divorces—fathers gone,
the custody arrangements, stepparents.
But one sick kid, not even in my group,
tormented me and everyone in sight.
All kids aren't cute—Matthew was proof of that:
his porcine face went red when he got mad,

his beady eyes would disappear, his lips
thrust out to pout, his teeth like tiny rocks.
One day I had him in my room to make
tissue dolls with pipe cleaners for arms.
He lingered after other kids had left,
refused to put the scissors down. I yelled
his name three times, and still he wouldn't stop
playing with the scissors like a plane,
running when I tried to grab his hands.
I had him by the collar when my boss
walked in to separate us from our clinch.
I thought I'd lose my job, but Peter said,
Don't let that little bastard drive you mad.
Days later everybody learned the truth—
the kid was acting out because his mom
was pregnant with another child, and Matthew
couldn't stand to share. We all prepared for
more tantrums when the kid was born, more hate.
But Matthew came to camp, picture in hand,
stroking the photograph with sticky hands
as if it were a toy he'd never break.
His baby brother's face looked just like his:
piggish and infantile, mouth a red wail.
This is my little brother, Matthew said.
He whispered it so softly I was stunned,
his pouty mouth gone soft with care and pride.

MY POSTHUMOUS MOTHER

She likes that I have a state job, well-paying,
even if the state isn't New York. Working
for the city, any city, is just too hard,
too few benefits for the work.

She likes that I'm married, even if
my husband isn't black, not Caribbean,
wonders when we're going to stop
fooling around, get down to business
and make her some grandbabies—
half-white, half-black, she doesn't care.

Disappointed that I don't go to church,
or read the Bible, or think of Jesus,
she'd trade a few textbooks for hymnbooks,
wants me to pray more, put my palms
together, lift my face to the Lord.

Always a bargain-lover, she's glad to hear
what we paid for this house, likes that
I put money away in savings, never touch it,
letting interest accrue on cash in case
of catastrophe, illness, death.

She's sad that I don't vacuum more, dust
more, that I let crusty dishes settle
in the sink for days, that I have forgotten
everything I might have learned
watching her at the stove, her hands
busy with chicken, rice, peas, water,

callaloo, yams—whatever made the house
fragrant. Sad to see me eat out so much,
she says she'd rather see me cook up
a savory meal of rice and pigeon peas,
pan of stewed chicken, meat
so soft it falls from the bone,
marrow ready to be sucked.

She likes hearing about my students—
their excuses, dramas, little victories.
Patients, students—not much difference
in her view—her hospitals and my
universities both needed to sustain us all.

She reminds me to go to the doctor,
take my vitamin, carry tissues in my
purse, to have spare change for the bus
or subway, to walk with my umbrella
on overcast days, keep two pairs of gloves
in winter, to try to learn to drive,
though she never did. *Wake each day
grateful*, she says, *for what you have.*
I wake each day glad to have been
her child, sorry that I cannot bring her
a cup brimming with warm tea,
a little sugar and milk making it
sweet enough to start the day.

RAVENOUS

I want chocolate all over my fingers,
melted and smooth so I cannot resist
licking the tip of each finger
as my palm's heat melts the candy.

I want popcorn with real butter,
popped in a pan, not a microwave,
salt sprinkled on each kernel,
not settling to the bottom of the bowl.

I want cheese—not processed cheese food,
but real cheese—Monterey Jack and Gouda,
Edam and cheddar, entire wheels of brie
melting and waiting for my cracker.

I want crackers. I want to crush
my crackers with my fists and leave a mess
I won't clean up until tomorrow—
a profusion of dirty dishes, cooked-in pots,

bowls with cake batter clinging inside.
I don't want anything steamed or lite
or low-fat. I don't want to eat
Healthy Choice meals, taking them

for their hideous green boxes and dumping
them in the trash instead, jeering the tiny
portions that look nothing like the meals
on the boxes. I don't care if my arteries

clog with fatty sludge—tonight I want grease
and fat and salt, real granules of real sugar,
no Equal or Sweet'N Low for this tongue,
this hungry body, ravenous mouth.

DOMESTIC HUMILIATION

What would my mother say if she could see
the piles of clothes growing larger, more frightening
in the corner of my bedroom, a bedroom that's not
really a bedroom, but a living room, the bed too big
to go up the narrow stairs? What would she say

about the disarray of books and papers and magazines
that any visitor could find in piles around my bed,
yellowing scraps billowing around the floor lamp—
bank receipts, business cards, the torn envelopes
of recent correspondence, forlorn without their letters?

Would she run one accusing finger over every
bookshelf, don white gloves to shame me into dusting,
leave me coupons for furniture polish, extra-strength
pine-scented disinfectant? I want to know what
she would do, wish I was through mourning her,

so I could clearly hear her advice about reheating
leftovers, polishing tarnished silver, making gravy.
If I could get done with this grief, I'm sure I could
remember where she said to keep lettuce so it doesn't
morph into a brown rock, what she said about getting ink

out of fake silk, how she'd turn frosty chicken breasts
out of shrink-wrapped packages. If I could be less
selfish, more attentive, I could recall little details—
whether boric acid really defeats crafty roaches,
which stains get bleach, which detergent. Instead,

this apartment grows dirty in ways I didn't think
possible—dark rings in the bathtub eluding my
scrub brush, ants on the counter marching merrily
past. Until I can learn to hear what she once said,
I'll be here: grief mine, floor unwaxed, mop dry.

BIOGRAPHICAL NOTE

Allison Joseph lives in Carbondale, Illinois, where she is a professor of English and director of the MFA Program in Creative Writing at Southern Illinois University. She serves as poetry editor of *Crab Orchard Review*. Her books include *My Father's Kites* (Steel Toe Books), *Trace Particles* (Backbone Press), *Little Epiphanies* (Night-Ballet Press), *Mercurial* (Mayapple Press), *Mortal Rewards* (White Violet Press), *Multitudes* (Word Poetry), *The Purpose of Hands* (Glass Lyre Press), *Double Identity* (Singing Bone Press), *Corporal Muse* (Sibling Rivalry Press), and *What Once You Loved* (Barefoot Muse Press). Her most recent full-length collection, *Confessions of a Barefaced Woman*, was published by Red Hen Press in June 2018.